Perspective on LDS Women's Ordination & Abuse

(Note this conversation was recorded on Aug 8, 2022, in Park City, Utah. The interview has been edited for clarity.)

Introduction

We don't usually discuss current events on *Gospel Tangents*, but we're going to make an exception. Jennifer Roach is a former Anglican pastor, and experienced sexual abuse from her Baptist clergy as a teen. She has a unique perspective on the latest AP News article about a sexual abuse case in Arizona. She is also a counselor, and we'll get her opinions on the case. We'll also get her opinion on ordaining women in the LDS Church. Does she support it? I think her answers will surprise you. Check out our conversation...

Tags: Gospel Tangents, Rick Bennett, LDS Church, Latter-day Saints, LDS Church, Mormon, Mormon Church, Church of Jesus Christ of Latter-day Saints, Mormon history, Mormon, LDS Church, LDS, Church of Latter Day Saints, Jennifer Roach, Anglican Church, Episcopal Church, sexual abuse, Ordain Women, conversion story, AP News on sexual abuse,

Contents

Anglican Pastors Converts to LDS

Introduction

We don't often cover current events. But, we're going to do that today with Jennifer Roach. She's a very interesting person in that she has been a former Anglican priest who converted to the LDS Church. How does that work? We'll also talk about the recent case, the AP article about the church helpline that's supposed to help bishops, when they deal with abuse victims and that sort of thing. Could they do things a little bit better? We'll talk to Jennifer about that. She's actually a licensed counselor, and has her own experience with sexual abuse. Unfortunately, she was a victim back in California, so she'll talk a little bit about that, and about the current situation. She's definitely got some unique perspectives, both as a counselor and an abuse victim and so you'll definitely want to check this out.

Interview

GT 01:00 Welcome to *Gospel Tangents*. I'm excited to have an amazing woman here on our show. She's a former pastor, and now a Mormon. Can we still say Mormon? (Chuckling) So why don't you tell us who you are?

Jennifer 01:16 I am Jennifer Roach. I am a licensed mental health counselor. Before I joined this church, that's true, I was ordained as an Anglican pastor. I have a master's in divinity. I also have a master's in counseling or therapy.

GT 01:34 Okay. Well, this is great. Now I've heard your story before. I'm sure most of my audience has not. So, tell us about--so Anglican and Episcopal, those are kind of the same thing.

Jennifer 01:47 They're very close cousins.

GT 01:48 So which one's the more conservative?

Jennifer 01:51 Anglican?

GT 01:51 Oh, really? Oh, I'm surprised to hear that.

Jennifer 01:52 Anglicans in the United States are more conservative than Episcopalians in the United States, by far. But Anglicans in the United States are probably more liberal than Anglicans, like, in Africa.

GT 02:09 Okay, because they allow women pastors.

Jennifer 02:14 They do. It's contentious in some circles, still, but they do. Yeah.

GT 02:17 Okay. This is my American history hat. The Anglican Church was founded by King Henry the Eighth. Right? Then, during the revolution, we didn't want to be tied with the Church of England.

Jennifer 02:35 Correct. So, they changed the name to Episcopalian.

GT 02:39 So, in America, it was known as the Episcopal Church. But in England, it was known as the Anglican Church.

Jennifer 02:43 Correct. Then, it was John Wesley and his brother and others who--they were Anglicans, right around that time when the name changed. They kind of say like, "We need to be the circuit-riding preachers. We need to take the gospel out to the people." And that's not how Anglicans normally are thinking, right?

GT 03:04 This is like the Second Great Awakening?

Jennifer 03:06 Yeah, so, John Wesley comes out of the Anglican Church at this time saying, like, "Y'all need to be doing more to get the gospel to the people. We're starting our own thing." There you go.

GT 03:16 Oh, wow. Very cool. So, eventually, we won the war.

Jennifer 03:24 We did. I can report that as of today.

GT 03:27 So, Anglicans aren't terrible, anymore? They're still kind of a division between Anglicans and Episcopal, right?

Jennifer 03:34 Yeah. So, in the United States, people who call themselves Anglicans and not Episcopal, have deliberately walked away from the Episcopalian structure, in part because they will say things like, "Oh, we don't actually know if Jesus was a real person."

GT 03:35 That's what Episcopalians say.

Jennifer 03:53 Yeah, not all of them. Many, many of them love Jesus, and they're fine. But you also get a lot of that kind of stuff on the leadership. So, people who call themselves Anglicans in the U.S., searched out, they call them flying bishops, but, basically, they're foreign bishops who would oversee them. So, when I was an Anglican, my top a bishop was actually the Archbishop of Rwanda, who was a welcoming refuge for American Episcopalians who wanted to break away from the Episcopalians.

GT 04:25 Oh, wow.

Jennifer 04:25 They have their own stuff. That's a whole different episode.

GT 04:29 This is great. We're getting a Pentecostal perspective,[1] a Lutheran perspective,[2] and now an Anglican perspective.

---

[1] See http://gospeltangents.com/people/chris-thomas
[2] See https://gospeltangents.com/people/willie-grills

Jennifer 04:34 I actually grew up Evangelical.

GT 04:36 Oh, really?

Jennifer 04:36 Broadly Evangelical. It was only maybe in the last 10 years before I joined this church, that I was an Anglican.

GT 04:44 Okay. Well, very cool. So, because I remember in your story, you said you knew somebody who was LDS, and they talked about this scripture that you'd never heard of. Tell that story.

Jennifer 05:01 So, I was involved in a lawsuit in California,[3] and one of the reporters who was most writing about it, he's a member of the LDS Church. He and I had worked together a lot. There was a bunch of stories that came out, and so he and I were getting to know each other. I kind of had this sense of like, "Oh, I know, he's a church-going guy." I didn't know anything, really, much more than that. The lawsuit involved a church where I grew up that I sued for my sexual abuse. So, I took them to court and won. That church decided to give a response to the initial stories about this lawsuit in a sermon. So, the pastor chose for his text to use Moses, and his sermon really was awful. It was basically, "Well, Moses messed up and God seems to forgive him. So, when leaders mess up, we should just forgive them." I was angry about it. I was all worked up. The plan was, my reporter friend and I were going to talk later in the week after both of us had listened to this. So, we're on the phone, and I...

GT 06:17 So, the sermon was recorded or something?

Jennifer 06:19 The sermon was recorded. This was pre-COVID, but they still had their sermons online.

GT 06:22 Okay.

---

[3] See https://www.sacbee.com/latest-news/article212300809.html

Jennifer 06:24 So I'm telling the reporter, his name is Garth Stapley, by the way. He won some awards for his reporting on my issue. [He did a] fantastic, absolutely amazing level [of] reporting accurate, good, fair, honest. So, I'm telling him all the reasons, on and on and on and on and on. He says, "Yeah, you know, I didn't like that sermon, either, but for different reasons."

Jennifer 06:49 [I'm] like, "Really, you've got to tell me why."

Jennifer 06:53 He says, "Well, I have different scriptures than you."

Jennifer 06:58 It's like, "No, you don't. What are you talking about?"

Jennifer 07:03 "I have more information about Moses than you do."

Jennifer 07:06 I was riveted. I had to know what he was talking about. Unfortunately, it's the middle of a workday. He's working in a very typical newsroom, that open floor plan, all the reporters are sitting around. So, he's like, "I'm not talking about Scripture with you at work."

Jennifer 07:25 I said, "Okay, that's fine." I think as soon as we hung up the phone, I'm immediately texting him of like, "Okay, text it to me, then." He sent me a link to the church's website where I read the Book of Moses. That's the first Latter-day Scripture I ever read.

GT 07:42 Before the Book of Mormon.

Jennifer 07:43 Before the Book of Mormon. I had no idea what I was even looking at, but that's what I read first.

GT 07:47 So, this is interesting to me, because, I don't know. It seems like my experience is most pastors get at least some sort of knowledge of Mormonism. But it sounds like you didn't get any. Is that true? Because you're both an evangelical and an Anglican.

Jennifer 08:07 So, I grew up in the evangelical church in the 70s and 80s. *Godmakers* was shown in my church, every single year. We were taught, as children-- I lived in Modesto, California. That's where I grew up. It's a fantastic place to grow up. We would drive into the bay area where the Oakland Temple is, near there. If you've ever seen the Oakland Temple, it's up on a hill, all lit up. You can see that thing from all over the Bay Area. What our leaders taught us was, "Don't even look at their temple, because evil things happen in there and you don't want to get corrupted, so like avert your eyes." So, I got plenty, a healthy dose of Mormon equals bad. But I also was childhood friends with a family who were members of the Church and I loved them. Their home was good and peaceful to me. I wanted, like, their mom to be my mom. So, I had a kind of a soft spot in me where I was always going, "These two pieces of evidence don't quite fit together, what my church is telling me and what I see in my friends."

Jennifer 09:19 In childhood and into my teenage years I didn't have any ability to sluice out what that meant for me. After adolescence, after childhood, even, those friends were out of my life. I had moved and by then I was mostly in evangelical circles. I went to an evangelical University.

GT 09:38 Biola?

Jennifer 09:41 No, I went to Seattle Pacific, because I was living in Seattle. Seattle Pacific was fantastic. I really enjoyed it. It's a really small school, but it was great for me. My M. Div. is from an Evangelical Divinity School, the Seattle School of Psychology and Theology. It's a great program but very evangelical. I have worked in churches, most of my adult life. So, my world became really insular in that sense. I can't even remember having a friend in the last 30 years who was a member of the [LDS] Church. I just have been around evangelical and Anglican church people my whole life.

GT 10:17 Wow. So how did you go from Evangelical to Anglican? Were you a pastor at an evangelical church before?

Jennifer 10:25 So, they wouldn't call me a pastor. They would title me Director in the churches where I worked, just because I was a woman. But I worked in evangelical churches. I was a children's pastor for a long time, did youth ministry, did family ministry, I did all kinds of stuff, right?

GT 10:40 Evangelicals don't give women the priesthood, either. Is that why?

Jennifer 10:42 Some do and some don't. It's church by church basis. The Evangelicals make the rules for themselves. So, churches that want to, do, churches that don't [want to,] don't. The evangelical world was good to me in some ways. They taught me how to read Scripture. They taught me how to love the Bible, and I still do. But the way evangelical faith kind of gets practiced is it's about an inch deep for most folks. It's really, really, broad. It's only about an inch deep. That just, ultimately, wasn't very satisfying to me. I actually went to Divinity School, not with the intention of, hey, I'm going to go get ordained, but with the intention that just said, I need to make sense of what it is that I have been handed in this Bible, in this tradition. I took two years of Greek and Hebrew. I learned homiletics. I learned hermeneutics. I learned philosophy. I learned all this stuff, just in part, because that's how my brain worked. I didn't get that kind of stuff in my churches, growing up.

GT 11:53 Interesting. So, you got your M. Div. at Seattle Pacific. You went back to Modesto and were kind of a children's pastor?

Jennifer 12:02 No, I actually, I lived in Modesto, up until the time was about 23, maybe 24. Then we moved away. I haven't lived there since.

GT 12:10 Okay.

Jennifer 12:11 So, college happens later in life for me. At age 31, is when I went back to school.

GT 12:24 After you already had your M. Div?

Jennifer 12:26 No, I started at community college at age 31.

GT 12:30 Oh, okay.

Jennifer 12:31 So, essentially three and a half years to get my BA and M. Div. was four years on top of that. Then, my graduate degree for counseling is three more years on top of that.

GT 12:35 Wow.

Jennifer 12:35 So, no, I don't have a doctorate, but I should. If I would have been smart, I would have figured that out.

GT 12:52 Oh, wow. So, once again, how did you go from evangelical to Anglican?

Jennifer 12:59 The evangelical church just wasn't satisfying anymore. Anglicans are deep thinkers. [They] understand a lot more about nuance in history and philosophy and how to actually understand Scripture. Whereas with Evangelicals, you get a lot of, "Just love Jesus, and it's going to be okay."

GT 13:17 Okay.

Jennifer 13:18 So, mostly my intellectual needs led me there.

GT 13:23 Okay, and so how did you become a pastor?

Jennifer 13:29 Well, I'd been working in churches almost my whole life. I mean, the first paycheck I ever got from a church, I was 17. So, a lot of these roles I had had were director roles, which means you're a girl pastor. So, when I came to the Anglicans, ordination is the entryway into doing any kind of pastoral roles. They have an entirely different theology of what it means to be a pastor. So, ordination is required. There's some testing that happens with that. There's some interviews. You have to have a master's in divinity.

GT 14:09 Which you already had.

Jennifer 14:10 Which I already had. Honestly, very often I could sit at a table with 10 Anglican friends with two master's degrees, seven years of graduate education and I would be the least educated person at the table.

GT 14:25 Wow.

Jennifer 14:25 So they are hyper educated. That's just the bar to-- if you want in on the conversation, have an M. Div., get ordained.

GT 14:34 Wow. So, you felt called to do that?

Jennifer 14:39 I did. I loved it. They were very, very good to me.

GT 14:42 And you did that for 10 years?

Jennifer 14:44 I did that for about 10 years. I was happy. I had, literally, no intention of going anywhere. And then I read the Book of Moses. I don't know what to tell you.

GT 14:56 (Chuckling) And that converted you right there?

Jennifer 15:00 No.

GT 15:01 You didn't even need Moroni's promise?

Jennifer 15:02 I didn't even need Moroni. No, that did not convert me on the spot. It was a process, and I took lessons for about nine months. Most of the time, it would be me, the two girl missionaries, who I wanted to be teaching me, because that was my personal preference, the two elders who were actually the elders assigned to the actual ward, where I lived, and, frequently, two senior-adult, missionaries. I think they were feeling a little nervous, because I had questions, and the kids didn't always know what to do with them. My friend, the reporter, would join us online, so he was in our lessons on Zoom. Often, somebody from the ward, the Relief Society President or whoever [would be there.] So, there would be like 10 or 12 of us sitting around for my lessons. We did that for months and months and months and months.

GT 15:51 Yeah. It would take some talking to...

Jennifer 15:54 I kept a notebook and just wrote down every single question I had, and I wasn't going to make a movement until my questions felt answered to me. I also, you know, after I read Moses, I read all of the Pearl of Great Price. I read all of the Book of Mormon. I read cover to cover, I read all of those long before I got baptized. I had many, many questions for my reporter friend, who is a saint for taking it, because it was like daily. "What about this? What about this? What about this," and the fact that he hasn't unfriended me yet is only attributed to his patience and goodness, not because I have any restraint whatsoever.

GT 16:39 So, polygamy wasn't a big deal to you.

Jennifer 16:41 I mean, it's a complicated issue. However, my point of reference on polygamy is the Old Testament. Everybody's a polygamist in the Old Testament.

GT 16:51 Exactly.

Jennifer 16:52 Who cares? So, I walked into the LDS polygamy situation of like, "Okay, it's a little bit more recent, but I don't, exactly, understand why all of you are so upset. I have come to understand and I have gotten a nice education. I know, I understand why people are upset about it. But I'm not. That's also another episode.

Women & Priesthood

GT 17:17 I'm sure you probably had to ask about--well, women and priesthood, right?

Jennifer 17:20 Women and priesthood, absolutely.

GT 17:21 I mean, that had to be a big deal for you. Right?

Jennifer 17:24 The day that I sat in an LDS service and watched the boys serving sacrament, is when I had the real realization of, that boy's 12, maybe 11. I'm a full-grown woman, a completely over-educated adult woman who has all kinds of power and responsibility, and that boy has more than I do in this context. That took a minute. However, if you asked me, "Do I want women to be ordained?" Hard pass.

GT 18:00 Oh, really?

Jennifer 18:00 Hard pass. We can talk about that. But that's where I'm at.

GT 18:03 Well, let's talk about that. That's where I wanted to go, because I can imagine that would have been incredibly difficult for you. How did you overcome that?

Jennifer 18:14 Well, I mean, it was difficult. There are different versions of difficult. The initial version of difficult was, I mean, maybe that's prideful, or maybe anybody in my position would have felt a little bit about like, "Wait, what, if I join all of you? I'm losing an awful lot," right? I have current friends in this Church today who are fighting for their lives to get women to be ordained, right? And here I am voluntarily giving that up. So, the personal piece was one part. The social piece is another part, though, which a lot of LDS women don't understand what it's like to be an ordained person in another denomination. So, my initial forays into that conversation, there was a disconnect for me around, well, only some people are ordained in the evangelical church. You get a handful, four or five, maybe 10 people in a church who are ordained. Nobody else is. Compared to the LDS Church, every eligible man can be [ordained.]

Jennifer 19:23 So, presumably, if women were ordained, every eligible woman would be presumably, and that's a different setup, and how does that end up actually playing out? I don't know. But in the evangelical world where women are ordained, even in the churches that fully 100% accept and support them, they face an incredible, incredible backlash, sexist, awful, awful comments from their own congregations because of their gender. That is no cakewalk for any of them. The pushback is intense. So, part of why that was easy for me to overcome was, I know what's on the other side of that, at least the evangelical version of it. And I am not eager to sign up for that again, right? The theological piece I got through by saying, I mean, it's, it's not a super sophisticated way to think about it, but, like, "Okay, if this is true, and then this true, and then this is true, I can understand how not ordaining women is true." If you don't have all these other things before it, it doesn't make sense. But in this larger context, it makes sense to put aside my own pride. I can put aside the social piece, whatever, and it becomes okay for me. But it was a struggle.

Jennifer 20:50 I'll also say this. Not all of them. And if this, if this doesn't apply to you, women, then, it doesn't apply to you. But in our church, in our LDS Church, one thing I have noticed is more than I would expect, women who say, "I'm so mad women don't have the priesthood. I'm so mad, I don't get to lead. When is all of this going to change?" It is baffling to me. Because you don't get out of the confines of a system by necessarily getting the system to change for you."

Like as a woman who's saying, "I'm so mad at those mean men that aren't giving me permission. I'm just going to sit here and wait for them to give me permission." Do I seem like a woman who is struggling to get her voice heard in this church? I don't. Do I seem like a woman who is struggling to not lead in difficult areas? No, I do not. I feel completely free to do whatever I need to do.

Jennifer 21:59 What women can fall into--you know, our culture has done a really good job about talking about toxic masculinity, this sort of over aggressive, "It has to be my way, and nobody else can be right," kind of... We've done a really, really good job of identifying that. What we've don't a less good job at is identifying the female version of that, which is not an over aggressive, "I have to have my way." It's an over passive, "I have to sit back and wait to be given permission to lead. I have to wait to be given an official title to lead." Because there seems to be this thought of, "If I'm given an official position, if I'm given an official title, and then I try to lead, I'm more guaranteed to be successful. I'm more guaranteed to not be criticized. I'm more guaranteed to just be universally loved." That's not a leadership is about. If you want to stick your neck out, then stick your neck out, but you're going to take your lumps, too. It is harder for women who are caught up in a toxic femininity, not all women, not most women. If this doesn't apply to you, it doesn't apply to you. But that's one of the problems I see, like women complaining they can't lead. Well, I'm not sitting around complaining I can't lead.

GT: You just lead?

Jennifer: I just lead. There's plenty of evidence of me doing that. I've been criticized for it and of sometimes been wrong and of getting things wrong. [There are] things I wish I had said differently. Bla bla bla bla bla bla bla, right? That's the risk that comes with it. What are you going to you do?

Jennifer 22:27 Well, it's funny because my experience. I have a couple of sisters. Both of them have said, "I don't want the priesthood." It's funny to look at the Community of Christ. I don't know how familiar you are with them.

Jennifer 23:55 I am.

GT 23:56 You know, in 1984, they allowed women to be ordained, but they don't allow every man to be ordained, either.

Jennifer 24:04 Yeah.

GT 24:07 That's not how they function.

Jennifer 24:08 They're a weird hybrid.

GT 24:10 Yeah. So, a third of their first presidency are female. A third of their apostles are female. They have patriarchs and matriarchs. Is that a more appealing model to you? Is that more like the evangelical model you're used to?

Jennifer 24:31 It is more like the evangelical model I'm used to. It is not a more appealing model to me. There's a Community of Christ congregation in Seattle. It's actually not far from where I live. I've been aware of it, since I was investigating the Church. I have never given serious emotional consideration to joining with them. I think I mean, maybe there are ways in which I would align with them better. But, that's not who my people are.

GT 25:00 I mean, I know one of the things that they say is, they don't like that every man gets ordained, just at the drop of a hat. And [they think] that there should be a little bit more discernment, and for those women who don't want to lead, they shouldn't lead. And for those men who don't want to lead, they shouldn't lead, which is very different from LDS. But, to me, it's kind of interesting, because it does allow people like my sisters to be, "Well, I don't want to lead. I don't want to be the bishop. I don't want to.. I'm fine with being a Relief Society president or Young Women's president or whatever."

GT 25:40 So, it's more accommodating in that way. I do think, well, since Kate Kelly got excommunicated, the Ordain Women crowd has gotten a lot quieter.[4] They're still there.[5] The website's still out there. They're still trying to promote it. But they're not trying to be as confrontational as Kate was. So, there are some of these militant feminists, I guess, but I don't think they're representative of all women, of all Mormon women.

Jennifer 26:13 Yeah.

GT 26:15 The ones I go to church with, I mean, I don't talk a lot about that, I don't talk at all about this at church. I only talk about people like you.

Jennifer 26:24 Don't do that.

GT 26:26 I would suspect that if there were a revelation, like 1984 with the Community of Christ, Mormon women would probably go along with it. They go along to get along. They're not seeking this out. Some are, but I think they're a minority.

Jennifer 26:46 Yeah. I think there are so many opportunities for leadership in areas I am interested in. It is hard for me to imagine that other women can't figure out ways to lead in the areas they are interested in. I understand that I bring some strengths to the table. I bring education, I bring some of these other things. In the distribution, maybe I'm in the tails, right? However, I've been in this church for three and a half years. Do I seem like I'm struggling to lead? No, I do not.

GT 27:23 You've been on several podcasts. I know you've been on *Leading Saints*[6] at least twice.[7] What other podcasts? You have you been on *Mormonland*,[8] I believe.

---

[4] See https://gospeltangents.com/2019/05/ordain-women-leadership-part-4-of-5/

[5] See https://ordainwomen.org/

Jennifer 27:32 Oh, yeah, I did Mormonland. I gave a FAIR talk[9] two years ago. They interviewed me about that. I can't remember all the ones. I mean, I've done a bunch. There's people who are probably like, "Oh, this lady again?" And then there are other people who are like, "Who is Jennifer Roach?"

GT 27:49 Yeah. So, it must have been hard, because you had to change career paths, right? You go from being a pastor to...

Jennifer 27:59 Not as hard as you might expect.

GT 28:02 Okay.

Jennifer 28:02 Because by the time I was already, like, before I ever even read the Book of Mormon, I had credentials in both. So, I was actively working in churches. But I also had a therapy practice. I had worked full time as a therapist before that. So, it's not like I had to quit my job, and then all of a sudden go and get retrained in some other field. I had both masters to draw off of, and I'm not the sole income earner for my family. So, that also makes it easier. I know folks who the faith transition question is completely out of the question. They're like, "Well, it might be interesting to find out about your church, but please don't tell me, because if I'm interested, I can't do anything about it. Because I've got five kids, and I'm the only one in our family who earns income and I'm a pastor, so I'm not changing."

GT 28:54 Yeah.

---

[6] See https://leadingsaints.org/4-reasons-why-bishops-should-be-meeting-with-youth-an-interview-with-jennifer-roach/

[7] See https://leadingsaints.org/reporting-abuse-church-helpline-the-bishop-an-interview-with-jennifer-roach/

[8] See https://www.sltrib.com/religion/2020/08/19/mormon-land-therapist/

[9] See https://www.fairlatterdaysaints.org/blog/2019/12/28/from-anglican-minister-to-relief-society-sister-interview-with-jennifer-roach

Jennifer 28:55 That was not my path.

GT 28:56 Okay. So, it was a little bit smoother, because you could go into counseling, which you'd already been doing.

Jennifer 29:02 Yeah. Easy.

GT 29:03 Okay. That's interesting. So, talk a little bit more about patriarchy. Is this problem in the LDS Church?

Jennifer 29:24 Let me try and use the language of the feminist world that would be talking about the patriarchy, right. If the patriarchy is a problem, or to the degree that it is a problem, it is also a problem to sit and say, "Well, I demand that the patriarchy give me permission, or endorsement to lead." Like, why not subvert the system, in a sense, lead where you want to lead? Maybe you don't have a title. Maybe you don't have an official position and I understand the arguments for why those are so important to have, I'm not pretending I don't understand those.

GT 30:05 Let me ask you this, because, I talk with a lot of different Mormons schismatic groups. David Ferriman,[10] he's got the Church of Jesus Christ in Christian Fellowship. It's kind of an internet church. One of his selling points is you don't have to leave your church to join my church. So, he has told me, and I don't know who these people are, but he has told me that there have been women in the LDS Church that wanted priesthood and he's given them what he calls the Magdalene Priesthood, which is similar to the Melchizedek priesthood, so that they can ordain other women or lay hands on the sick.

Jennifer 30:46 Sure.

GT 30:47 I've heard. I've been to Sunstone. I've heard about women who have laid hands on the sick. Now that used to be a

---

[10] See https://gospeltangents.com/people/david-ferriman/

practice up until the 1950s. Then, the said, "No, if there are elders around you should call for elders." Would it be okay for a woman like this to say, "Well, you know, I've been listening to Margaret Toscano,[11] and Michael Quinn,[12] and they say, due to my endowment..." Although you were at the FAIR conference a few days ago.

Jennifer 31:15 I was.

GT 31:16 There was a woman who said, "Due to baptism, that women have priesthood, and, at the time, lay hands on the sick." The prophet hasn't endorsed that today. But would it be okay for a woman in that situation to say, "Hey, by virtue of my endowment," let's at least go there, "I can lay hands on the sick."

Jennifer 31:38 Can she lay hands on the sick and pray to Heavenly Father to heal them? Absolutely. Can she pray for her own children? Absolutely. Is that the same thing that is what is purported to be happening when an elder does that? No. Does that mean it's meaningless and pointless, and that praying to God, that shouldn't matter? Of course not. In our church, there are women who have put their hands on me and prayed for me, but nobody pretended it was a blessing. Right? So, the idea that like, "Oh, women are barred from this kind of care of each other." That's ridiculous. Nobody's going around pretending that it is what it isn't, "So, now I have some kind of priesthood authority here to do this." It's a, "Brother and sister in Christ, and we all are praying to our Heavenly Father," kind of authority. I'm not going to go as far as to say that's identical to, "I already have the priesthood." I think that's a ridiculous argument. But, if I had a friend, and she was pregnant, yeah, I'm going to put my hand on her belly and pray for her. And I hope the elders don't put their hand on her belly, right? Like, yes,

---

[11] See https://gospeltangents.com/2021/08/spiritual-eccles-priesthood/

[12] See https://gospeltangents.com/2018/08/women-have-priesthood-since-1843/

yes, I am. Am I blessing her? Am I acting in any priesthood role there? No.

GT 33:01 You're just doing it as faith.

Jennifer 33:03 Just doing it as faith. I mean, if people have a problem with that, that's nonsensical to me. What is the problem with one woman praying for another woman? I mean, there's obviously like, it's very, very conservative people who might have the problem with that. On the other side are people who would say, "Oh, like you actually, you're acting in function as priesthood right here. You might as well name it that." Well, no, I'm not.

GT 33:29 Well, the other issue comes up is like if a woman has to confess a sin to a male Bishop. That can be very intimidating. The question is, why couldn't she confess those sins to a female Bishop? A male is going to ask different questions, probably more invasive questions than a female. So, why should a woman have to submit to a male authority in those situations?

Jennifer 34:03 Yeah, so this comes up with me with clients quite a bit, actually. Probably half my clients are members of the church, and people will talk about something in therapy that ultimately becomes an issue they want to turn away from and are struggling to do. I, as their therapist, am more than happy to talk with them. We can figure out what the blocks are to changing their behavior. We can figure out strategies for behavior change. We can figure it out philosophically. We can do all these things. But I can't do what their bishop can do. If we had female bishops to confess something to, the same would be true. I can't do what your female bishop does. We don't have that. I'm certainly not advocating for that. So, your bishop brings something to the table that your therapist doesn't. The Relief Society president doesn't. That's how the system is set up. That is how it is. I'm okay with that. I know plenty of people who aren't. And I'm okay with them not being okay with it. Like, I don't judge them. I absolutely am fascinated by their perspective. I, at the end of the day, I just don't share it.

Should Clergy Meet with Teens?

GT 35:18 Well, and it's interesting, because, you've kind of touched on this, and I would love you to share as much as you're comfortable with. Because you mentioned earlier that you were involved in a sex abuse lawsuit with a Baptist pastor. Is that right?

Jennifer 35:34 Yep.

GT 35:36 And there's the whole issue with Sam Young. Kids shouldn't be talking to the bishop without parent present, or whatever, which has changed.

Jennifer 35:46 Yep, it has.

GT 35:47 So, can you talk about this issue? Is it okay for a woman to be alone with a bishop and confess sexual sins? Is that a way for grooming to happen?

Jennifer 36:04 Well, first, let me refer back to two years ago, I gave a FAIR talk[13] on this. It didn't focus on adults, but bishops and teenagers. So, if you want the longer answer, that's a 45-minute talk. If the question is, is that a way, potentially, for bishops to groom people? Of course. However, I'm going to change and talk about teenagers, just because this is where I've done the research more.

GT 36:34 You've had unfortunate personal experience, as well.

Jennifer 36:40 Adults in every other church that exists are also talking with teenagers about sex. There is no church, where teenagers don't need to talk about this as a subject. How does sexuality fit in with my faith? That is an appropriate developmental task for them to figure out. What happens in a lot of churches, I'm going to talk mostly about evangelicals, is that the youth leaders,

---

[13] See https://www.fairlatterdaysaints.org/blog/2019/12/28/from-anglican-minister-to-relief-society-sister-interview-with-jennifer-roach

who sometimes are trained, usually there's one trained person and then a whole bunch of volunteers. So, they're not any more trained than LDS people are. The volunteers will pull a kid aside, "Hey, gosh, let's talk about what's going on with you and your boyfriend or let's talk about what's going on," you know, whatever, "with your porn viewing." They have those conversations with kids on the regular without informing the parents. Parents never know about those conversations.

Jennifer 37:01 In our church, the bishop meets with the kid. The parents certainly knows that that's happening. It's probably scheduled. There is no, "Hey, let me pull you aside for a little private conversation, and oh, by the way, I'm never going to tell your parents we discussed graphically your sex life." So, is there a danger there? Of course, there's danger there. It's better than—it's safer than in other places. It's not as bad as it could be. There is no risk-free way to live in the world. What are you going to do, lock kids in their homes? They're actually more in danger in their homes when it comes to abuse. It's family members and close friends of the family that abuse most often. Lock kids out of their homes and just keep them at school? 24/7? Well, there's your second biggest source of sexual abuse is schoolteachers. So, we send our kids to school. We let them live in our home. Those are high risk activities for children. But there is no way to live in the world without risk.

GT 38:43 So, do you support the new guidelines where a parent can be in there?

Jennifer 39:01 Absolutely. Right? If the kid wants them in there, if the kid wanted their youth, their young woman's leader in there with them, that's allowed. If the kid wants a friend with them, that's allowed. Of course! whatever is going to make that kid feel more comfortable. However, what I don't love is when parents insist that they must be in there and the kid disagrees. There is a role to be played…

GT 39:11 Because there could be abuse in the home.

Jennifer 39:29 Yeah, because that kid might need to confess something that their parents—not confess, but reveal something their parents are doing. They also might need to reveal some activity that they themselves are involved in that the parents don't know about, yet. The [church leader is in the] role, kind of the aunt or uncle figure plays in the church of like, "I'm not your parents. Like I'm not going to ground you if you reveal something to me. We can talk about it and we can figure out how to go talk to your parents together." That is an important role. So, If the kid wants it, 100%. I'm suspicious if it's dad that wants it.

GT 40:07 To make sure that…

Jennifer 40:07 I am sorry to say that, but it's true.

GT 40:09 To make sure that nothing gets said that gets him in trouble, or whatever.

Jennifer 40:10 Is against his dad.

GT 40:12 Have you had these, especially when you were a pastor, I don't know if I should use the word explicit, explicit sexual conversations with young boys?

Jennifer 40:24 Let me think. As a pastor, not likely. How the evangelical church is set up is, usually, there's one person who has something like the title, youth director or youth pastor, but they, alone, are not taking care of the youth. They've got a whole crew of volunteers underneath them, men and women. For the most part, the men are going to be having conversations with the boys. I don't think I ever had, in my role as a pastor, certainly as a therapist, but that's different.

GT 40:59 Okay.

AP Sex Abuse Story

GT 41:00 Because this all kind of leading into this AP story.[14] Let's talk a little bit about the helpline. There's a big thing out here. There's a terrible story in Arizona, where a father was sexually abusing his daughter, and it went on for at least seven years.

Jennifer 41:23 It's horrific. It's the worst case I've ever heard of in my entire life.

GT 41:28 So, there's this helpline that bishops are supposed to call. Now, the way the Church frames it is, "We have a lay clergy. These are marketing majors and construction managers, they're not psychologists, like you, generally speaking.

Jennifer 41:46 I'm not a psychologist, I'm a therapist.

GT 41:47 A therapist.

Jennifer 41:47 A psychologist is a PhD or Psy D level.

GT 41:50 Okay. They're not therapists like you, that are that are used to dealing with these sorts of things. So, in theory, it sounds like, "Hey, let me call the Church. They'll help me with this." And that sounds like a great idea. But, the problem, at least in this Arizona case, is it looks like the Church said, "Don't call authorities," and from what I understand, there's a little bit of a gray area in Arizona about whether you can call authorities. But this bishop was instructed not to call the authorities.

Jennifer 42:31 It's unclear if he was instructed not to call or that it was up to him, if he called. I have not gotten clarity on that.[15] I don't

---

[14] See https://apnews.com/article/Mormon-church-sexual-abuse-investigation-e0e39cf9aa4fbe0d8c1442033b894660?taid=62eba8c09fe1e80001bd50e3

[15] Jennifer clarified in an email: "Late last night {Aug 8, 2022} the AP released video of the Bishop Herrod, in his own voice, saying that the helpline told him he was not allowed to call, his hands were tied. He then goes on to say that he passes this information along to the next

think that there's a document that reveals [that.] I'd love to know if there is. Did they tell him, "Do not call?" Or did they tell him, "There's an out and you can take it, if you want?" I don't know.

GT 42:49 I'm going to look up something here in a second.

Jennifer 42:51 Please do. I would love to see it.

GT 42:52 But, at any rate, so the criticism is there's a clergy exemption in some states.

Jennifer 43:03 Twenty eight states or something.

GT 43:06 I thought—was it a clergy exemption in 28 states? I thought it was 28 where they were mandatory reporters,

Jennifer 43:11 I could have it backwards. There are many states where there's a clergy exemption. Arizona is not the only one.

GT 43:18 Well, because, I heard you mention this on the Oregon case, which is another case, and I kind of want to talk about that. My

---

bishop. This is a helpful piece of information to have as previously it was unclear what he was told. It helps explain why the bishops did what they did. But questions remain. The primary one I'm concerned with is, "Why did the system break down this time when it's worked well so many times before, and how do we fix it?" But I also think it's fair to point out that this 9 min video is intended to give an emotional punch. Every visual image, piece of music, and word spoken is carefully chosen to drive home the same emotional point. It's actually rather well done if that is the goal. But they certainly are not going to include any information that takes away from their point, including things the Bishop may have said that show a wider view of what happened. We get 1 short quote from him and nothing else. It is also fair to mention that an Arizona Grand Jury took up this question last year in case GJ21-0072. They asked, "Did the bishops do anything legally wrong?" and while their conclusions are secret, we can observe that as of today the bishops have not been charged with any crime. "

understanding is Oregon is a mandatory reporting state. So, the bishop did what he was supposed to do. He reported the sexual abuse. The wife of the husband, who went to jail for sexual abuse is,,,

Jennifer 43:41 She's suing the church.

GT 43:42 She's suing the church, because the church reported, but the church was following the law in that case. So, I don't think the case has been settled yet.

Jennifer 43:50 I don't think it has either. I tried to find an update on it and just couldn't.

GT 43:53 Yeah, I looked for it last night, too. I don't think this woman has much of a leg to stand on, personally. I mean, I'm not a lawyer.

Jennifer 44:01 It wasn't thrown out. I'm not a lawyer, either. But it wasn't thrown out.

GT 44:08 Because I know that the question is, in some states, you're a mandatory reporter, and you call and it sounds like the Oregon Bishop did the right thing. In Arizona, it sounds like it's a little bit of a gray area, you can or cannot. From what I've read, it sounds like the Church said, "Do not report this." The idea is, from the Church point of view, we don't want to have splashed in the newspaper, "Oh, Mormon accused of sexually abusing his daughter." It sounds like the church is scared of bad publicity, instead of "Hey, bishop in Arizona, go call the police and tell them what's going on." Because this went on for seven years. I don't want to say--and the church is defending this, that the bishop did nothing wrong, because he followed the helpline.

Jennifer 44:55 Like in a very technical sense, he did nothing wrong.

GT 44:57 But, morally--the church is not about legally. We're not supposed to take alcohol and tobacco, which are perfectly legal things to do in America. But morally, in the LDS Church, they're not supposed to do that. So, why in the world would it be--and I realize these are lawyers and they have a lawyer thing. But, from a moral point of view, why isn't the helpline telling this bishop in Arizona, "Get the police in here, now"?

Jennifer 45:31 Let me be very, very clear upfront. Those bishops should have called full stop. However, for some reason, it made sense for them not to.

GT 45:47 Most likely the helpline said not to, don't you think?

Jennifer 45:51 Well, that's one very possible, very probable piece of this. Let me actually back up a little bit. There are folks that want to say, [that] the bishops should have called. There's nothing else to talk about here." And that's fine, like that's an opinion. You can hold that opinion.

Jennifer 46:13 Some people kind of go the next step into interpretation. The bishops should have called. They didn't. This is proof. This is evidence that the church is evil." Okay, you can do that, too. But you also can take the same facts, the bishops should have called and they didn't, and instead of saying, "Well, the church is evil, say, "Okay, let's get curious about what are the factors involved?" The helpline is one of them. But there are also some lack of clarity of, "What, exactly, did they know, when?" In the Arizona paperwork, there are very few times when the bishops are even mentioned. They're not the center of this. So, they get very few mentions, and when they do, it's often with statements of like, "Adams revealed that he was abusing his daughter," in one. What exactly did he reveal? Because there's a wide variety of behaviors this guy is doing, all the way up from raping her and filming it, to--he filmed her while she was changing without her knowledge, even filming her with her knowledge, whatever.

Jennifer 47:21 What along that path did the bishop know and at what point? I'm not trying to defend them by any means, but to say [that] there are more factors at play here. It's just trying to understand what happened, so that hopefully, we can figure out how to do better. It doesn't seem helpful to say, "It looks like the helpline did this. Story closed and nothing else to talk about here." I would much rather say that okay, there are pieces involved here. One of them is, in the court paperwork. There is testimony from a lot of people. One of them is the FBI agent called Jay Allen. He has a quote. I just want to make sure I say it right. This is him, talking to the court, repeating what he knows about the mom's meeting with the bishop. He says, "During the free talk," that is, the wife's conversation with the FBI, where she was just allowed to tell her story. "She said that there was a time when during an interview or discussion with her bishop that she was asked where the line was? How far is too far?"

Jennifer 48:34 She said, "If Paul ever touched any of my children, then I'm going to leave him." So, at times, abuse is being disclosed, and at times we have statements like this, where she is acting like abuse is not going on. She knows perfectly well, even at every juncture along the way, that it is. But what is the bishop supposed to know from that? "If Paul ever touched any of my children, I would leave him." It is reasonable to see a way that the bishop understood that as, "This child was not actively being abused. Mom would take the kids and run." The court also says the judge says in no other case has he ever seen a woman who had more opportunities to rescue her own children than this woman. Her husband was gone for months at a time for work. She has a very large family who loves her and supports her, who would gladly have evacuated her and hid her from him. She had an entire ward begging her to let them help her. She doesn't do anything, and in fact she lies continually. She tells the FBI that she has lied about things and then continues to lie about things. I am not saying the bishops did the right thing. They should have called. However, it is understandable to see why they were confused.

GT 50:07 Well, I guess my concerns, and the concerns expressed by those in the Twitterverse...

Jennifer 50:18 Oh good grief. I haven't had time for Twitter. I've read the court documents. I'm not reading Twitter.

GT 50:23 Well, the idea is, maybe I should read a couple quotes here. Elisa at Wheat and Tares wrote an article on August 4, that said, "Stop Protecting Sexual Predators."[16] She quotes from the AP article. The idea is, I don't want to get into the details of what the bishop knew or didn't know. It's more of the helpline, because it says, "The article reports that the sealed records say calls to the helpline are answered by social workers or professional counselors who determine whether the information they receive is serious enough to be referred to an attorney with Kirton McConkie, a Salt Lake City firm that represents the Church. But, it also says in capital letters that those taking the calls, 'Should never advise a priesthood leader to report abuse.'" That sounds terrible, right?

Jennifer 51:21 It's not what the handbook says.

GT 51:22 But this is what the, let's see, the sealed records in the helpline...

Jennifer 51:29 So, let me help out a tiny bit here. Those sealed records are not about this Arizona case.

GT 51:37 No, they're about a West Virginia case. But he's applying that to the Arizona case. Because doesn't it seem pretty applicable? Like this probably is what happened.

Jennifer 51:48 Sure, that's how that reporter made those cases. There are two issues here. One, they're sealed records. I haven't

---

¹⁶ See https://wheatandtares.org/2022/08/04/stop-protecting-sexual-predators/

seen them. You haven't seen them. Nobody's seen them. The court officers and participants in that case have seen them and the reporter has seen them. Is he reporting that correctly? I don't know. I have incredible respect for that reporter. There is no one better on this topic than him. So, I'm not criticizing him by any means. The issue that I have is, you can't pull information out of one case and always automatically apply it to the next case. Is that applicable here? I don't know. Maybe it's one of the pieces of the pie that needs to be looked at.

GT 52:22 Okay. Anyway, it continues on, "Counsel of this nature should only come from legal counsel." It continues on, "Two church practices identified in the sealed records work together to ensure that the contents of all helpline calls remain confidential. First, all records of calls to the helpline are routinely destroyed." I mean, that sounds like destroying evidence.

Jennifer 53:01 Well, let me ask you a couple questions. When was that the policy of the helpline? When are these calls from? What year is this Arizona case even talking about? We have no idea.

GT 53:13 Well, it says they're routinely destroyed. So, it does say, earlier, that it was set up in 1995.

Jennifer 53:19 So, this West Virginia case, is it an abuse case that happened in 1995, and those were the early policies of the helpline? Or was this a 2001 case, and that's still the policy? Is this an old case, and it's changed? We don't know any of that?

GT 53:37 Okay.

Jennifer 53:37 So, do I love the thought of like, the evidence gets destroyed at the end of the day? No, I think that's terrible. I think that should change. Is that their current policy? I don't know.

GT 53:47 Why would it change unless there were public pressure to change it?

Jennifer 53:50 Well, things change all the time without public pressure to change them.

GT 53:55 It doesn't seem like the Church changes all the times without public pressure.

Jennifer 54:01 I don't know.

GT 54:02 Okay.

Jennifer 54:03 I'm just saying it's an open question on the table. That's not defending abuse. That's not defending this dude. That's just, like, this is a reasonable question.

GT 54:13 This is a question that, I mean, as you mentioned earlier, this reporter is the same one who uncovered the Catholic Abuse scandals.

Jennifer 54:20 He is extraordinary. Top Notch.

GT 54:23 We probably wouldn't question him on those issues. So, it seems reasonable that he's probably on the right side of the issue here.

Jennifer 54:32 Except for that he needed those West Virginia documents to make a connection that you do not see that connection in the Arizona documents. There's just not enough information about the Helpline in them, for him to have gotten where he gets, and so he's reaching back to these West Virginia documents. I love a good document leak. I would love to see those documents. But are they describing the Helpline as it exists today or 25 years ago?

GT 55:01 It certainly is describing--do we know when this West Virginia case was?

Jennifer 55:05 That's the question. Literally, no one knows.

GT 55:08 Okay.

Jennifer 55:08 Well, at least, at this point in the West Virginia case and everything was sealed. So, it doesn't seem like the Church has a lot of incentive to change their practices. I mean, it continues on. "The notes are destroyed by the end of every day." Like, every day we destroy our notes? [This quote was] said [by] Roger Van Coleman, the Church's Director of Family Services, in an affidavit included in the sealed records. Second, Church officials say that all calls referred to Kirton McConkie lawyers are covered by attorney-client privilege and remain out of reach of prosecutors' and victims' attorneys. The Church has always regarded these communications between its lawyers and local leaders as attorney-client privilege," said Paul Rytting, the Director of Risk Management." The question is why is this in Risk Management and not in Family Services?

Jennifer 56:00 Well, because you don't want a therapist answering the phone. Do you know the McMartin preschool case?

GT 56:10 I do. But for those people who don't know, tell us that story.

Jennifer 56:13 Mr. & Mrs. McMartin have a preschool in their home. When it's first revealed, it's considered THE most horrific child abuse case that exists. All these kids are confessing massively incredible, terrible sexual abuse. But what had happened was the children were interviewed by social workers. Social workers are not forensically trained in the collection of evidence or how to collect evidence, especially from a child, without leading them. And that is what happened in these cases. You can still go online and see the videos of the social worker interviewing the child. You can look now and be like, "Oh, yeah, I see how her holding up a doll with anatomically correct parts and saying to a two-year-old, "Show me what happened." And he yanks on the doll like... Well, I understand how the social worker got there. But that's not how you forensically interview a child.

GT 57:11 Right.

Jennifer 57:11 So, the kids give really, really bad information because it got collected in a really, really bad way. Therapists and social workers have their role. You want an attorney answering that phone call for the protection of those victims, because those initial disclosures of what actually happened, whether they're coming from the victim themselves or a close confidant like a bishop, those are incredibly important. They need to not be corrupted. They need to be collected in a certain way. I'm not trying to do any of that. Neither are any of my therapist peers. So, is there a time and a place for a therapist in this helpline situation? Absolutely. But not answering the phone at first.

GT 58:01 Well, the issue is, supposedly, this guy confessed to the bishop that he was sexually abusing his daughter. It sounds like and I don't know so, I can't say this, for sure. But it sounds like the Church Helpline said, "Don't contact authorities, "and this continued to go on for seven more years through another Bishop and another child.

Jennifer 58:28 Yeah, so technically, it goes on for three years. Between Bishop One and Bishop Two, there's a three-year span. He's excommunicated after three years. Abuse goes on for four more years, which is horrific, and, yes, we bear some responsibility in that. But he was not in the church for seven years. He was he was excommunicated after three years.

GT 58:49 But most people are going to say, "Who cares?" I mean, I guess in the eternal scheme of things, that's a big deal, but…

Jennifer 58:58 The kid's still got abused. It's horrific.

GT 59:00 The kid's going to be abused for three more years that that person could have been in jail. I mean, he's since committed suicide, so maybe he would have committed suicide sooner.

Jennifer 59:13 We bear responsibility for that. We, our church has made those girls lives harder. Whatever settlement they get, they deserve every single cent. And one is quoted in the AP article as saying how much she hates Mormons and they're the worst people in the world. She's absolutely allowed to say that. And we should be humble enough to say, "We are going to listen to you."

GT 59:43 That's what people are so upset about is the Church is more worried about its reputation than this poor little girl.

Jennifer 59:48 Here's the part that I found really frustrating with that, is the bishops didn't call and they should have.

GT 59:54 But they were probably directed not to call.

Jennifer 59:56 And they were probably directed not to call, like, let's even go to there.

GT 1:00:00 That's the systemic issue that people have an issue with.

Jennifer 1:00:03 The interpretation, though, that says the Church was worried about the publicity and didn't want, "Oh, Mormon dad is abusing his Mormon kids." That's an interpretation. Is that the motive of what was going on?

GT 1:00:16 What else would it be?

Jennifer 1:00:17 This was an incredibly complicated situation. Many people involved in this case, know that something is odd, they know enough to call, and none of them call, either. This isn't "Mormon Bishop is the only guy in this family's life that knows what's going on." There's a woman. She is a border patrol agent. She also attended the church. She's the children's Sunday School teacher, and she's the visiting teacher for the mom. She's in their home enough to know that something is wrong here. Something is wrong with these children. And when dad comes home from being out of town for a time, the kids fall apart. Right? That alone, in my profession, certainly in hers, is enough to call. She didn't call. But she didn't call the Helpline to say, "Should I call the police on them?" and [have] the church tell her "No. Don't." She didn't call because there were a lot of factors at play.

Jennifer 1:01:18 Here is one of them that I think has not been well talked about, and it's really sad. It's incredibly, incredibly heartbreaking. The mom in this family is very mentally ill. She's incredibly mentally ill. Her brother testifies that she has an entirely flat emotional life, so that she has the same emotions at the birth of her child, as she does at the molestation of her child. That's not normal. There's a lot that is broken in her psyche. She had gone through her own abuse. He, the husband is certainly abusing her. He tells her week one of being married, "You have sex with me when I want, or I rape you."

Jennifer 1:02:00 She's been in this marriage for quite some time by then. So, it is understandable. But mom changes her story. They're being abused. No, they're not being abused. They're fine. I actually can manage it, because I have taken care of the situation, and everything is fine. Here's what she tells the FBI agent and her bishop at some point. "I manage this by having rules. The children, especially the girls are not allowed to be alone with their father. The girls are not allowed to sit on his lap. She changes that later to the boys and the girls are not allowed to sit on his lap. I want to be careful how I say this. She on the autism spectrum. The vast majority of people who have autism, it does not lead them to enable the abuse of their children. I'm not saying that. However, the version of autism that she has, has this hyper-control element to it. She has a very real belief--it's wrong--but it's a very real belief in her mind that if I can make the right rules, all of this will stop and get taken care of.

Jennifer 1:03:06 She destroys one of her husband's phones that he uses for recording all this, at one point. If I destroy the phone, then it stops. Well, that's any...

GT 1:03:15 Just get a new phone.

Jennifer 1:03:16 Right? Any adult understands that's ridiculous. You are in magical thinking. You are not in the world of reality right now, if that's what you think is going on. And that's where she was. It takes even her therapist; her therapist is interviewed by the court. It takes her therapist months and months and months to realize we're not just looking at anxiety and depression here. Something else is going on. How was the bishop supposed to figure out there's a mental health case here that is really complicating what she's able to tell us? It's not a defense.

GT 1:03:48 Well, I mean, to me, back to the to the confession, when the man confessed to the bishop, end to the story. And all these other things that happen after the fact don't matter.

Jennifer 1:03:57 Do you know what he confessed? Do you know what his actual words were?

GT 1:04:00 What was it?

Jennifer 1:04:01 I don't know. It's not in any of the court paperwork. There's no way to know. Did he say, "I am actively filming my daughter while I'm actively raping her," or did he say, "Gosh, every once in a while, I peek around the corner while she's getting changed." Both of those things he did. We don't know what he confessed. I would love to know.

GT 1:04:22 Well, even if he's spying on his daughter, wouldn't that be a call to the police?

Jennifer 1:04:27 It would be. The outcome, obviously, is going to be quite a bit different. One of the problems you see in this family, which, frankly, you see in a lot of abuse situations. I deal with this as a therapist. Someone will tell me such and such as happening. Okay, we need to make a CPS call. You call CPS, you tell them all this stuff. Well, they go and interview that person. And it is very common/ It's the expected case that abuse victims get scared, and they change their stories. So, I can't tell you how many times I've had clients say, "Oh, my therapist, she's a liar. I never said that." And it's understandable why they do that. Well, that you see this mom doing that.

GT 1:05:09 Well, even Elizabeth Smart, she had opportunities to escape. And they're in survival mode. So, I don't want to blame any woman for any way they react to these because...

Jennifer 1:05:16 It's Understandable. Correct.

GT 1:05:21 Because none of us have been in that situation. Unless you're Elizabeth Smart, and you know, or unless you're Jennifer Roach, because YOU know, sometimes you're in survival mode. She [Elizabeth] lied to the police.

Jennifer 1:05:35 Repeatedly [Mrs Adams], and that she tells them I'm lying, and then she keeps lying. I'm not blaming her in any sense. However...

GT 1:05:40 It makes it hard to prosecute.

Jennifer 1:05:42 This case, you start looking in the court documents, and absolutely nothing is as it appears, at least as seen through her lens or the lens of anyone who's repeating what she said. Because it's this and then, no, actually, it's this and then no, actually it's this. Here's an example. What did he get excommunicated for?

GT 1:05:59 I don't know.

Jennifer 1:06:01 The assumption is for the abuse of his children, right? What she says is he's excommunicated for having sex with his mother.

GT 1:06:15 Whatever. That's still a terrible reason.

Jennifer 1:06:18 That's still a terrible thing. Did that actually happen? Did she just make that up? In her mind trying to protect her kids or him or something?

GT 1:06:28 Probably.

Jennifer 1:06:29 Who knows? Maybe he actually did have sex with his mother. He was conducting multiple affairs and abusing his own children. This is a depraved man. Maybe that's in the realm of possibility. But we don't know. We don't know why he got excommunicated, the actual reasons.

GT 1:06:43 Because the Church won't put it out.

Jennifer 1:06:45 I would love it if it were available, and I bet that they would get sued over that if they put that out. I'm not defending. I'm not an apologist for abuse. The bishops should have called. We all wouldn't be here if they had.

GT 1:07:00 Yeah, I mean, I think that's just the thing. It just seems like, and maybe this is a stereotype, but the Church can fix this stereotype, I think, by putting in the handbook, because it seems like you said there were some states where they were not supposed to [report.]

Jennifer 1:07:21 I wish I would have said this clearer. I said this to Kurt,[17] and I said this in a couple of other places where I think I said it in a way that made it seem like some states have it so that you cannot [report.]

GT 1:07:32 Yeah, that's what it sounded like.

Jennifer 1:07:33 [That] you're legally barred. And that's not true. That's not-- I don't know of any--if someone knows of a state, I'd love to know. But there are states where...

GT 1:07:42 There are 46 states where it's either mandatory or optional for clergy to report.[18]

Jennifer 1:07:46 Yeah, and I think the remaining states don't have a, "We'll legally prosecute you, if you report." Right? However, the states that have a clergy exception, have a clergy exception. Was that the wise thing to follow in this case, looking back from everything we know now? No. What did the bishops know? When did they know it? They haven't spoken. I don't imagine that we will hear from them. It's completely unclear in the court paperwork what exactly they knew, when because they're not the focus of it. I would love to know that. It just should be an open question, instead of saying, "Oh my goodness, that bishop knew from day one, that this little girl was being raped. And then he just sat on his hands and did nothing for seven years." That's not what happened.

GT 1:08:33 Yeah, a former bishop on Facebook posted, "In my experience, the first two things that were never part of any

____

[17] See https://leadingsaints.org/reporting-abuse-church-helpline-the-bishop-an-interview-with-jennifer-roach/

[18] For more detailed info, see https://www.childwelfare.gov/

conversation, the entire call centered around making sure that I, as an ecclesiastical leader, didn't say or do anything that would put the Church in legal jeopardy." Now, this is a person who has been a bishop within the last 10 years. "I was told not to talk to law enforcement and that if law enforcement happened to contact me about the situation, I was to say that I was, 'Represented by counsel' and to direct them to the Church's law firm. I was offered no advice or resources for how to stop the abuse or how to help the victims. When I asked about those things, I was told to talk to my stake president who was the one who told me to call the Church's helpline."

Jennifer 1:09:23 That's a failed system. It should not have happened like that.

GT 1:09:26 "With absolutely no training in this sort of thing, whatsoever, I had to figure out, on my own, how to get help for various members of the family. It was gut wrenching."

Jennifer 1:09:36 Yeah, of course.

GT 1:09:37 And so, this is within the last 10 years, and this is a former Bishop. I know some bishops have had good experiences. But there was a Twitter thread about a bishop in Texas who had a good experience and did everything they said and got help for the victims. But, in this Arizona case, the bishop condemns that sort of reasoning.

Jennifer 1:10:02 I am not comfortable saying here, "We know exactly what he was told on the help call." We actually don't know that. The Church hasn't said,[19] and the bishop hasn't said. It's nowhere in the court paperwork. Except for there are some secondhand people saying, "We think that the helpline told him not to call." It's all hearsay. It's not firsthand. I would love to know what actually happened, so we could actually deal with what it is. I think

---

[19] Likely because the records were destroyed.

probably the biggest pushback on what I'm saying here is people want to move from, "The bishop should have called, and he didn't, therefore Church bad." Right?

I want to say, "The bishop didn't call, and he should have. Let's look at all the many, many factors here, figure out what exactly happened and went wrong. And let's try and fix it and build a stronger church. Right? Because the Bishop should have called and didn't, church bad. That doesn't really change anything.

GT 1:10:57 Well, the people who are doing this are saying that Kirton and McConkie need to say, "Call the police, today. Don't wait."

Jennifer 1:11:04 I wish they would have.

GT 1:11:05 And that's the systemic change that needs to happen.

Jennifer 1:11:01 Yeah, there are a number of breakdowns in all of the systems that should have served these kids, and that is absolutely the top of the list. But it is not the only one. And when we say, "The bishop should have reported. He didn't. Church bad." We stop right there, and don't look at all these other pieces.

GT 1:11:26 I don't think people are stopping there. They're saying this needs to be changed. And we need to change to protecting the victim.

Jennifer 1:11:31 The only glances I have given at Twitter, have people saying, "Two bishops molested the same girl."

GT 1:11:39 I haven't seen that.

Jennifer 1:11:40 So, do you think people are reading very carefully? No. Twitter is a dumpster fire. Read original documents.

Learn how to source documents. Learn how to evaluate a source. Stay off of Twitter.

GT 1:11:51 (Chuckling)

Jennifer 1:11:52 If you want to find out what happened, you're not going to find it on Twitter. Go learn how to read original documents.

GT 1:12:00 Well, cool.

How Do Young Abuse Victims Disclose?

GT 1:12:01 Well, have we beat this to death?

Jennifer 1:12:03 Let me see if there's anything else I want to say. Can we talk a little bit about what abuse disclosure actually normally looks like for kids?

GT 1:12:13 Okay.

Jennifer 1:12:14 So one of the issues that comes up in this whole Arizona case is a lot, a lot, a lot of folks saying, and I think from a pure and good heart saying, "Well, I would have noticed the abuse and I would have reported it."

GT 1:12:26 I don't agree with that. For one thing I was telling you off camera about a situation that I know of where I was completely unaware of sexual abuse going on with somebody that I considered a friend.

Jennifer 1:12:41 Yeah.

GT 1:12:42 And so anybody who wants to play Monday morning quarterback, sorry, when you're on the field, it's completely different.

Jennifer 1:12:48 There is an incredible amount of that. I had a really good friend, who has been a bishop in the past, write to me and say, "I would have done what the Helpline told me to do."

GT 1:12:58 Exactly, I probably would have, too.

Jennifer 1:12:59 Right. I think most people would have. Here's sort of part two of that. Adults have a belief, almost universally, that a kid or teenager who wants to reveal abuse is going to make some kind of appointment with you, sit down in your office and say on November 7, at 2:38pm, here's what my dad did to me, and it's illegal and here's my entire," blah, blah, blah. That's not how children or adolescents confess abuse. It is extremely rare. There are some who did. I actually ended up, when I very first talked about my abuse, I kind of bread crumbed. I told a male Pastor. That was my choice, and I kind of breadcrumbed him into it. We had maybe a dozen conversations before I got to the point to say, "Here's what happened."

Jennifer 1:13:51 So, when kids confess something, they do it one of two ways. One is they do the breadcrumb method, and they'll say something that they know is a little off. They know, it's the tiniest little bit of the iceberg, and they want to see what you are going to do, adults. And if you blow past it, they are not trying again with you. If you pick it up, and be like, "That's a weird thing to say. Tell me more about that." Then, maybe you get the privilege of 12 more conversations with them, and then they tell you what happened.

Jennifer 1:14:25 That's the standard. What I did is actually a little bit fast. The other way, and this is the vast majority of abuse that's revealed by children or teens is by accident. The kid says something that an adult can pick up on and the kid didn't know that what they said just revealed something. Here's my best example is a girl who says something weird to her Sunday School teacher that her dad knows all about her underwear. "Well, gosh. You're 11. What's your dad doing knowing about your underwear? You're a little old for that." That's the conversation that comes of like, "Weird, tell me more. Why does your dad know about your panties?"

Jennifer 1:15:09 But as adults, we're really afraid. Especially my heart goes out to men, bishops, especially, who get put in this situation. A kid drops some little nugget like that, in a youth interview. The bishop wants nothing more than to just move on to the next question on the list. Because he doesn't want to be the middle-aged creeper who has to lean forward and go. "Wait, what?" But that's actually what that kid needs. You want to you want to save kids from abuse, adults, you need to open your ears in a different way. This kid isn't going to sit down and tell you, "Here, let me give you the times and dates of all of my abuse and exactly what happened." They're going to say weird stuff. And kids say weird stuff all the time. So, you're going to get a lot of false positives, that you're going to go down on a trail. And if you're like, "Oh, that's just something dumb." The other piece is this. It is impossible to know what the state of abuse is today, whether in our church or in any other church. And here's why. If abuse happened in childhood or in adolescence, what do you think? When is the first age that a person might report that?

GT 1:16:26 How young?

Jennifer 1:16:27 Yes.

GT 1:16:28 Maybe 8, at the earliest.

Jennifer 1:16:30 What do you think is average?

GT 1:16:33 Probably 20.

Jennifer 1:16:35 According to Child USA who does work in this space of reporting and statute of limitations laws, the average age is 51 of first disclosure, 51.

GT 1:16:49 Wow.

Jennifer 1:16:50 Meaning, a 10-year-old kid who's being abused today, we are not going to know about her abuse for 40 years. So, are we doing better? Yes, I hope so as a society, and there's still stuff we don't know. There's still news happening that we don't know about. If adults could learn to listen to kids in a little bit different way, that number could drastically come down from 51 to maybe 21. I'm 51.

GT 1:17:22 Has the #MeToo movement helped with that kind of stuff?

Jennifer 1:17:25 That's an interesting question, because this statistic is actually pulled, I think in 2017 or 2018, which is just when the #MeToo stuff is beginning. So, probably. However, are we accurately catching that yet? Probably not. Because a lot of these cases are too old to report on, so people don't go report to the police. Like when this happened 40 years ago, they're not going to want to hear about it. So, it's complicated. We, as a church, we could do better with the Helpline. We could do better around policies. As adults in this church, we could do better at how we talk to kids and teenagers about abuse. We could do better about how we follow little suspicions. Can I talk about background reports?

GT 1:18:16 Yeah, go ahead. I know you talked about that with Kurt.

Jennifer 1:18:20 Yeah, you already know what I'm going to ask you. This man, he not only abused his own kids, he produced child pornography with them. He was consuming child pornography before he ever even had children. There's one comment in the court paperwork that he potentially had produced something, child pornography wise, before he even is married to his wife. So, he's got a long career at this. And he's a border patrol agent. You think the Church can do a better background check, than the Border Patrol can? The guy submitted to the most intense background check that there is.

Jennifer 1:19:00 So here's my example. If you're somebody who's running an after-school tutoring program, and Paul Douglas Adams sits down and says, "Hey, I love kids. I just want to help out."

The director of the tutoring agency is going to say, "We take child's safety very seriously here. You have to pass a background check first."

What's he going to say? He's going to say, "Sure, totally. Okay, let's pull up the paperwork."

And two weeks later, that background check is going to come back. He's clean. And she's going to introduce him to kids, and he is the most destructive child abuser that I know of. And she is going to sit back with some surety that that guy is okay. So yes. Should our church be doing background checks? Probably because you do catch the rare person who's already been convicted.

GT 1:19:51 I've heard that if you did--what do they have? The sexual predator list or whatever in every state; if you looked at that, you'd be shocked at how many people are your neighbors.

Jennifer 1:20:01 Yeah, absolutely. Absolutely. Right. There are people on that list, and we could find them with background checks. That is real. The person who says, "Well, why not just do them anyway? There's no harm in it." The harm, actually is that now Miss Director of After School Tutoring thinks Paul Douglas Adams is safe, and she lowers her guard a little bit. Could we be doing better as a church around issues like that? Absolutely.

GT 1:20:31 It's not foolproof.

Jennifer 1:20:32 So and so has taken the abuse training that you have to take in the church. All that means is he clicked through some buttons. Don't let that lower your guard down. There's a lot of changes that need [to happen.] It's not just the Helpline here. I can list 20 changes I want to see the Church make.

GT 1:20:04 Let's hear them!

Jennifer 1:20:05 Well, I mean, I've just been telling you about all of them. There are a lot of changes we can make. Putting the only emphasis on the Helpline, I get it. It's on the top of the list. However, you're much more likely...

GT 1:21:01 Well, I know some of these people are all for background checks.

Jennifer 1:22:05 There's a petition going around right now.

GT 1:21:07 Didn't California just make it the law...

Jennifer 1:21:06 California did, yeah. And so, the church in California, they will have to have background checks there. I am not opposed to background checks, as long as you understand what a background check is, and what it isn't. People seem to think that it's some kind of like, magic oracle that tells you if this person has ever done something in the privacy of their own home, and it's not. You have to have been not only charged but convicted. Paul Douglas Adams would have passed a background check until the day he died. Until the day he died!

GT 1:21:39 Now, he was the Border Patrol agent?

Jennifer 1:21:41 No, he's the father. He commits suicide in jail.

GT 1:21:44 Oh.

Jennifer 1:21:45 On the day he died, if someone would have background checked him, he that he would have come back completely clean.

GT 1:21:49 This is the Arizona father. Is that what you're talking about?

Jennifer 1:21:51 Yes. So, I get it. Yes, we probably should do background checks. That is a change that probably should happen. I just want to implore, do not let any policy make you feel safer than you should. People want a magic bullet and background checks or policies like having to do the training or the two deep rule, right?

People say, "Oh, well, all of these are going to guarantee. We can relax." Well, no, you can't. There is no magic bullet that 100% protects kids. Nobody wants to hear that. I don't want to hear that, either. But it's true.

Better Training for Clergy?

GT 1:22:34 What else do you have? Are there any other things besides that?

Jennifer 1:22:39 Oh, you know, I mean, the other thing that I think has not been well said is there is record in the court of the bishops were trying to get the mom to call the police. They were also trying to get the dad to call the police, which he was not going to do that in a million years. Right? They're trying to get the mom to do it and she wouldn't. So, there is some understanding from both of them, that calling the police is the right thing. What it is that blocked them from doing that? I don't know. We can speculate. But we don't have that document. If somebody has it, I'd love to see it. But it doesn't exist yet. So, the idea that they just didn't care--I mean, my very short peeks into Twitter are, "I can't believe two Mormon men just sat on their hands, knowing the girl was actively being raped, right at that moment." Like that's just inflammatory, and that's not what happened here.

GT 1:23:41 Right.

Jennifer 1:23:44 So, I don't know. That's probably more than anyone ever wanted to talk about abuse.

GT 1:23:51 Well, I think, I'm sure this is my first episode on abuse that we've ever had on *Gospel Tangents*.

Jennifer 1:23:58 Is that right? Oh, it might not be the last.

GT 1:24:03 Well, I'm trying to think. Is there anything else?

Jennifer 1:24:06 Nope. I think that's it.

GT 1:24:07 All right. Well, it's been so interesting. I love hearing--I might have to have you back on. We'll talk about biblical literalism. That sounds like fun.

Jennifer 1:24:17 Oh, there's so many fun things we could talk about. Someday, we'll see.

GT 1:24:21 But it's great. There's so many people that wonder how a pastor could convert to Mormonism. Jana Riess is another one.[20]

Jennifer 1:24:31 Yeah.

GT 1:24:31 She has a degree in divinity and she joined.

Jennifer 1:24:33 Or, I think more current to this situation is people wonder, how can you have your own abuse background, know all that you know about this case, and stay in the Church and keep faith?

GT 1:24:47 Right.

Jennifer 1:24:48 That is really the person that I'm interested in, is you can navigate these things. I'm doing it. It's hard. You're going to need support. You're going to need a good therapist and a whole bunch of good friends.

GT 1:25:03 Is that why you went into therapy? Was because of your own abuse?

Jennifer 1:25:09 I mean, yeah, after a while, you know your way around a therapy room. You might as well get the piece of paper that says you're allowed to do it. So, yes.

---

[20] See https://gospeltangents.com/2019/07/randomly-sample-mormons/

GT 1:25:17 Do you wish we offered better training for our bishops? One of the things that you said, which I thought was very interesting on Kurt's podcast, was, when you're an Evangelical, you don't get that much more training than a Mormon bishop.

Jennifer 1:25:32 Yes.

GT 1:25:33 And I was surprised to hear that.

Jennifer 1:25:34 Yeah, not on abuse issues. You get some. But mostly people who become pastors in the Protestant world broadly, and certainly in the Catholic world, they're bookworms. They're interested in learning dead languages. They're more comfortable in the library than in the social hall.

GT 1:25:58 What about, like, marriage counseling? Don't you get some training in that? Because that's a big part of being a pastor as well, right?

Jennifer 1:26:04 It is, but that's done from a very specific, like, here's what, in their case, the Bible, or here's what God might want you to do. That's not at all what we mean by what a therapist does. That's not what I do as a therapist. Right? They're acting as, "Let me be the deliverer to you of what God has said about marriage and how you should work at marriage." That's all they're doing. That's what biblical counseling is. So, yeah, they're doing it. They probably took one class in Div school.

GT 1:26:36 So, a couple that's having marriage issues, and they go to their bishop, pastor, priest, whatever. Should that bishop, pastor, priest, whatever, say, "I'll give you a few scriptures to read, but really, you should go get professional counseling." Should that happen all the time in every church?

Jennifer 1:27:01 It depends upon what the issue is. Bishops in our church--if you want to use the keys language--they hold specific keys. They don't hold the therapy key. So, they're going to have to outsource that. And I have received plenty of clients from bishops who have been like, "Hey, I know of somebody's good. You should go see her." But a person who is in trouble in some way, like without being able to say what is going on in the marriage, they might need a bishop and a therapist. A bishop does things I cannot do.

GT 1:27:35 Such as?

Jennifer 1:27:36 They're there to help with the repentance process. Therapists are not there to help with the repentance process. They're not there to help with confessing sins to God. That is not what therapists do. Therapists use empirically validated methods to help change thoughts and behavior. There's no conceptualization in modern therapy about what sin is. There's none. A person sits down and says, "I like to have sex with my cat." I don't even know how that--never mind. He comes to me, and he says, "I'd like to have sex with my cat." The first words out of my mouth aren't, "That's a sin, you need to stop this behavior." I'm going to try to understand how we got there. What were the things that made this develop? What's going on, that's keeping him stuck there? How [do I] help him move through that? None of that is conceptualization of sin or of forgiveness or of God or spirituality or any of those things. That's what a bishop does, and cat guy might need a bishop to do that with him.

GT 1:28:45 It seems like I've heard stories, where a woman, especially, went to a bishop, and claimed she was raped.

Jennifer 1:28:57 By the bishop, or by somebody else?

GT 1:28:59 No, no, by somebody else, and the woman had to go through the repentance process.

Jennifer 1:29:07 Yeah, ridiculous. Ridiculous. That shouldn't happen. That's number 17 on my list.

GT 1:29:14 If you have a bishop who's a psychologist, they're going to react very differently than a bishop who's an insurance agent, or whatever. It seems like there is a little bit of Bishop roulette. So, when we talk about the repentance process, could the Church, especially in this case of rape, could the Helpline better train and say, "If a woman comes to you and says she was raped, you don't say, 'What were you wearing? Did you enjoy it?'" You know, these kinds of really [invasive questions.]

Jennifer 1:29:49 Please don't ever say that.

GT 1:29:50 Because some of these bishops were like, "Well, I've got to find out exactly what happened. Were you wearing something inappropriate? Were you drunk?"

Jennifer 1:29:57 Yeah.

GT 1:30:00 I mean, there's a case of BYU where a girl got drunk and then got raped. And the Honor Code came after her. And so, shouldn't we do a better job of [not punishing the victim?] What do we do in those cases?

Jennifer 1:30:12 It's a little bit chicken and egg for me. Is that bishop flowing over their banks? They're not staying in their lane. Is that what this is? Or do people in the pews look at the bishop, as kind of a low rent therapist? They can't get into see a therapist, everybody's full, or it's a lot of money or whatever, I'll go see my bishop. And not that that person is necessarily like, telling the bishop, "I want you to also be my therapist," but they lead the conversation in a way that that becomes the topic. It's some of both, I'm sure. If I had my wish, bishops would be extremely clear on the gift and the skill and the keys that they bring to the table. Those are valuable and needed in the life of members. That is an incredibly important lane that no one else can occupy, please occupy that lane to the fullest of your ability. But, members, please stop asking your bishop to act like your therapist. Go get a real therapist. You might need both, somebody to help you with repentance and somebody to help you with thought patterns or behaviors or whatever.

GT 1:31:30 That's nice if you have good insurance, right?

Jennifer 1:31:33 Yeah, the United States and our mental health, that's a whole other episode.

GT 1:31:37 I mean, here's one other story. I've never told this ever. Gosh, how old was I? I was 20-21 years old. I was on my mission. I was a district leader, and so I had to interview somebody for baptism. In the white handbook, one of the questions is, "Have you ever had an abortion?" And if they say, "Yes," all it says is contact the mission president. So here I am. Let's say I was 21. I was probably 20 or 21. I don't know how old I was.

Jennifer 1:32:13 You poor 21 year-old self.

GT 1:32:14 I interviewed this woman. "Have you had an abortion?"

She says, "Yes."

I'm like, "What am I supposed to do now?" Because there's not a whole lot [of information on how to react.]

The next sentence is, "Call the Mission President." Yeah, like, am I supposed to just, like, abruptly end this interview now? And I didn't know what to do. So, as gingerly as I could, I kind of asked her. She was a young teenager and wasn't ready or whatever. And she was sorry about it. She wished it never happened. So, I was like, "Oh, I don't know if you can get baptized."

Then, she was like, "What? Really?"

GT 1:32:54 I was like, I need to call my mission president.

Jennifer 1:32:57 I hope she eventually got baptized.

GT 1:32:58 Well, let me finish. So, I called the Mr. President. I told him what happened. He asked me all the same questions that I happened to ask her. He said, "She can be baptized." I was like, whew! I was scared to death. Because there's no, I mean, 21 years old. There's no training for this.

Jennifer 1:33:17 Right, and part of me wishes that there were something and part of me says, "Absolutely not. You don't put that in the hands of a 19-year-old boy, you tell him to call the grown up." He doesn't need to have that conversation with her. Like, we're not going to train him how to have conversations about abortion with women.

GT 1:33:35 Well, who should be asking the question, because that's the question you ask if you're a bishop.

Jennifer 1:33:40 It still is. It was asked at my baptism interview. I wish missionaries were trained a tiny bit better on how to eloquently transition into, "Hey, we're just going to need to have a little bit more details on that. I need to loop my mission president in."

GT 1:33:56 I think that's what I did. But I was scared to death.

Jennifer 1:33:58 Of course you were. But I don't want a 19-year-old boy to sit there and decide, does she get to be baptized or doesn't she?

GT 1:34:04 Well, and she was really nervous. I remember.

Jennifer 1:34:07 Of course.

GT 1:34:08 I've just got to call...

Jennifer 1:34:09 Did she get baptized?

GT 1:34:10 She did. She did.

Jennifer 1:34:10 Yeah. In one sense, I understand that the dilemma of that. I know a lot of elders, and their brains are not yet mature enough to make that call. It's not their job. So, I'm really glad that that's what the handbook says. Call the grownups.

GT 1:34:31 Yeah, but there was no, "How do you finesse this? What if they say yes?" Because, up to then, everybody always said no. It was no big deal.

Jennifer 1:34:40 A footnote would be very helpful to everyone in that circumstance.

GT 1:34:43 "If they say, yes, this is how you handle it." And I think I did the best I knew how to do.

Jennifer 1:34:49 It sounds like you did great.

GT 1:34:50 And it worked out. But yeah, I mean, ugh.

Jennifer 1:34:53 I know. The whole point to all of that is therapy life and church life are different. You might need both. There are things that you can get from therapy that you can't get at church. There just are. And there are things at church and from your bishop that you can't get from therapy. And those two things need to work together in tandem, not checking on each other. They're two different entities. They're working on different goals. But, for a therapist to maybe be tempted to say, "Well, gosh, you don't need to talk to your bishop about this." They might. And it might be helpful for their spirit if they did. And for a bishop to say, "You don't need a therapist, I can talk you through this." Nope. Stay in your lane. Your lane is important. You're the only one who can be in your lane, be in it. My lane is therapy. There's billions, there's millions of us. Do your job, because I can't do your job.

GT 1:35:53 I just think the church could do a better job of, especially BYU with honor code. Rape is rape and no woman ever deserves that, or man.

Jennifer 1:37:04 Yeah, that's not a an honor code violation to be raped.

GT 1:37:09 And even if they were drunk, you know, they did something stupid.

Jennifer 1:37:12 That's an honor code violation, but getting raped is not. Right.

GT 1:37:14 Right. So, anyway, I don't know what else to say.

Jennifer 1:36:20 Yeah. I don't know how to land the talk. If we just keep going, it's going to grow into a million things.

GT 1:36:26 All right. Well, is there anything else we need to talk about?

Jennifer 1:36:28 Nope. That is it.

GT 1:36:30 Okay. Well, we'll have you back for a biblical literalism.

Jennifer 1:36:33 That'd be fun, anytime.

GT 1:36:34 All right. Well, Jennifer Roach, I wanted to say former pastor Jennifer Roach, thank you for being on *Gospel Tangents*.

Jennifer 1:36:42 Thank you for having me, really good questions.

Additional Resources:

Check out our other interview with Kurt Francom.

Kurt Francom on Church Leadership & Culture

Kurt Francom of Leading Saints podcast. He is trying to help LDS leaders create better culture around church history, faith transitions, & being LGBT friendly.

223: Do You Disagree with the Exclusion Policy?
https://gospeltangents.com/2018/12/03/disagree-exclusion-policy/

222: Should the Church Modify Bishop's Interviews?
https://gospeltangents.com/2018/11/30/church-modify-bishops-intvws/

221: Results of Faith Crisis Research
https://gospeltangents.com/2018/11/27/results-faith-crisis-research/

220: "We've Got to Have These Difficult Conversations"
https://gospeltangents.com/2018/11/24/we-must-have-difficult-conversations/

219: Ministering to the Faithful & Faithless
https://gospeltangents.com/2018/11/20/ministering-to-the-faithful-faithless/

218: Is it Bad to be Called LDS or Mormon?
https://gospeltangents.com/2018/11/18/is-it-bad-to-be-called-lds-or-mormon/

Lutheran Pastor's View of Mormonism

https://gospeltangents.com/2022/08/lutheran-pastor-interested-in-mormonism/

Rev Willie Grills Discusses Luther and Mormonism.

Willie Grills Rick!

Religious Violence/Word of Wisdom

Protestant Fights/Book of Mormon Churches

Religious Violence

Atonement Theories & Trinity
https://gospeltangents.com/2022/08/rev-grills-on-atonement-theories/

Story of Martin Luther, Grace & Works

Why is Lutheran Pastor Interested in Mormons?

Pentecostal Theologian Reviews Book of Mormon

Dr. Christopher Thomas teaches at Pentecostal Theological Seminary in Cleveland, TN. He's written "A Pentecostal Reads the Book of Mormon."

Final Thoughts

I hope you enjoyed our conversation with Jennifer Roach. Jennifer, thank you for sitting down with me and sharing your opinions. I think you've got some really good suggestions and I hope that we can improve and make society a better place, especially for abuse victims.

You can get our transcripts at our amazon.com author page. Just do a search for Gospel Tangents interview, and you should be able to find a bunch of them there. Please subscribe at Patreon.com/gospeltangents. Please subscribe at Patreon or on our website at Gospeltangents.com. For our latest updates, please like our page at facebook.com/Gospeltangents and also check our twitter updates Gospel tangents. Please subscribe on our apple podcast page https://tinyurl.com/GospelTangents, or you can subscribe on your android device. Just do a search for Gospel Tangents. Thanks again for listening. Click here to subscribe, here for transcript and over here we've got some more of our great videos. Thanks again.

Jennifer Roach

We don't usually discuss current events on *Gospel Tangents*, but we're going to make an exception. Jennifer Roach is a former Anglican pastor, and experienced sexual abuse from her Baptist clergy as a teen. She has a unique perspective on the latest AP News article about a sexual abuse case in Arizona. She is also a counselor, and we'll get her opinions on the case. We'll also get her opinion on ordaining women in the LDS Church. Does she support it? I think her answers will surprise you. Check out our conversation...

Rick C. Bennett is the host of Gospel Tangents and plans to use proceeds from book sales to put together educational materials that explore Mormon History, Science, & Theology. Please support the work by
1: Purchasing transcripts at Amazon:
    http://amzn.to/2DKTOEV
2: Subscribe at www.GospelTangents.com
3: Watch the interviews on our YouTube Channel
    YouTube.com/GospelTangents

Junaid KC & Divya NV